The Magic of Music

7 Imaginative Solos for Intermediate to Late Intermediate Pianists

Dennis Alexander

Foreword

I've always felt that music inspires magic, and everyone who experiences the joy of making music themselves develops the ability to discover this magic in one way or another. Perhaps it is that special feeling which occurs when a certain rhythm or colorful harmony touches the heart of the player; or maybe it is that favorite melodic line that inspires him or her to "sing inside" and feel the warmth of a beautifully turned phrase. The pieces in this collection are designed to entertain, teach and enhance the important musical and technical skills that are being developed at the intermediate level. I wish you much success and enjoyment as you journey through Book 3 of "The Magic of Music."

Dennis Alexander

Contents

This collection is dedicated to my friend, former student and musical colleague, Molly Morrison.

Moorish Gardens

Dennis Alexander

Moderato e molto amorevole

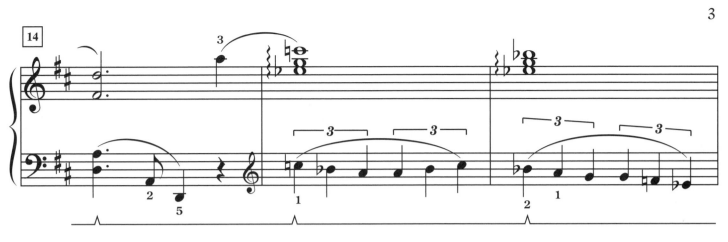

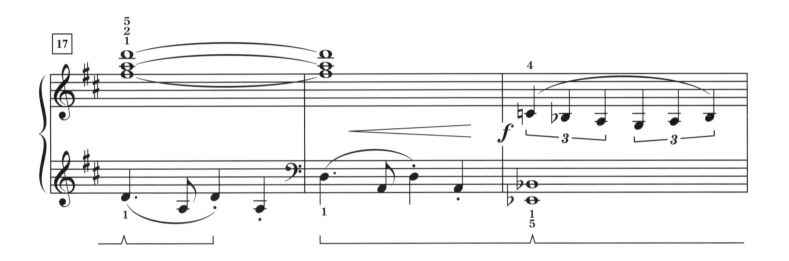

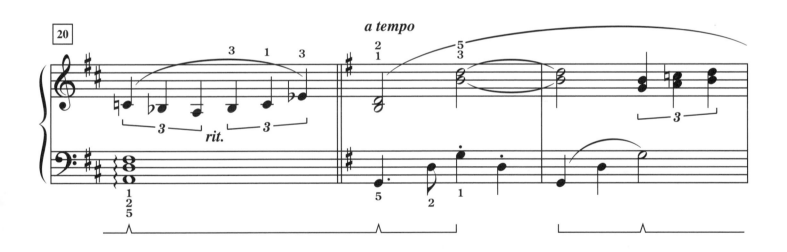

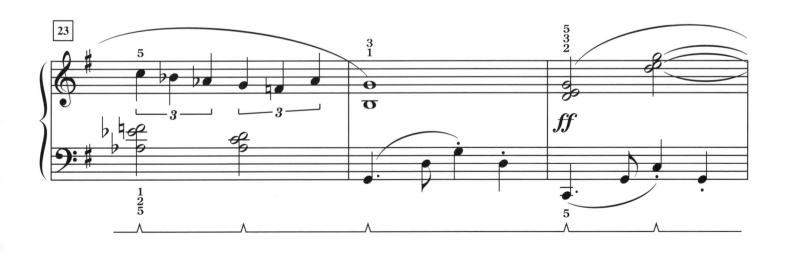

Like Yesterday

Dennis Alexander

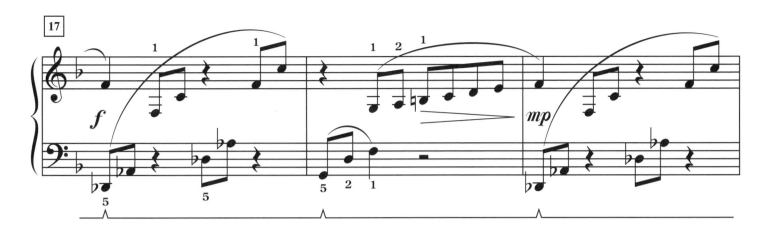

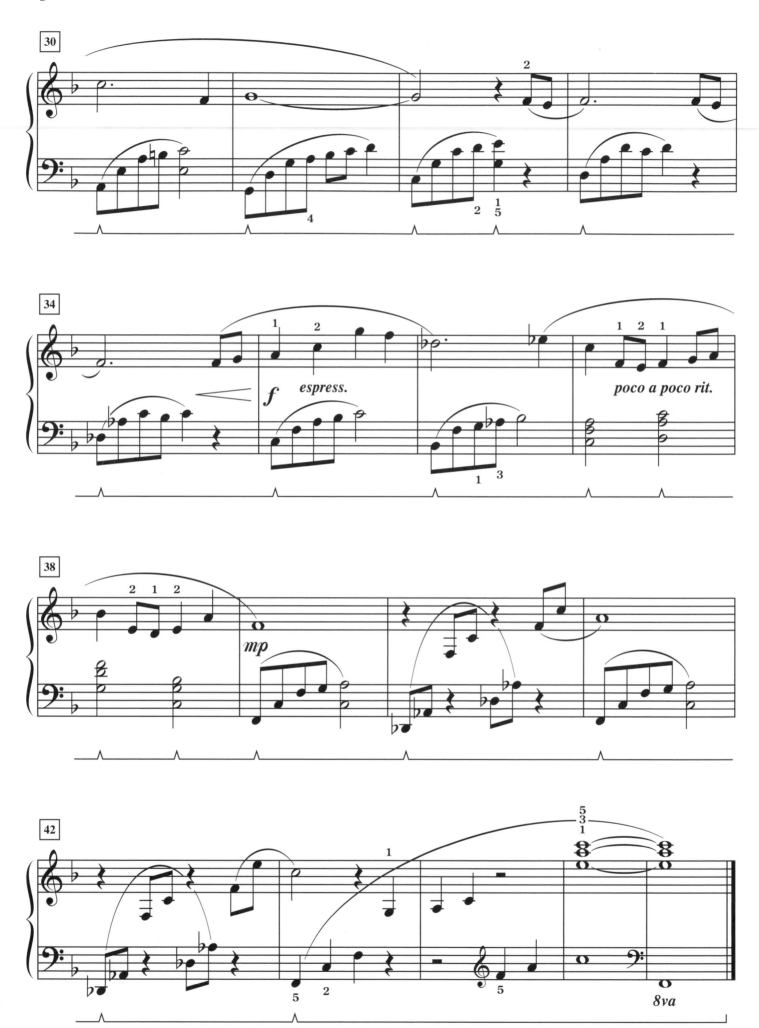

Give Me Five

Dennis Alexander

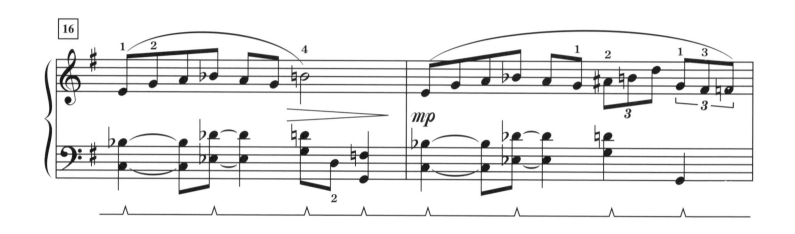

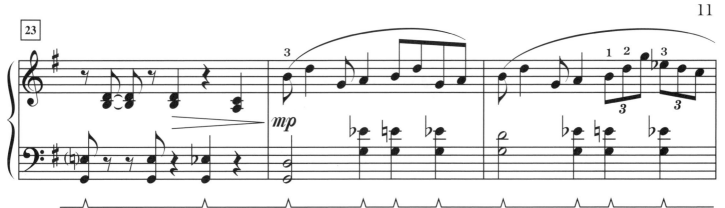

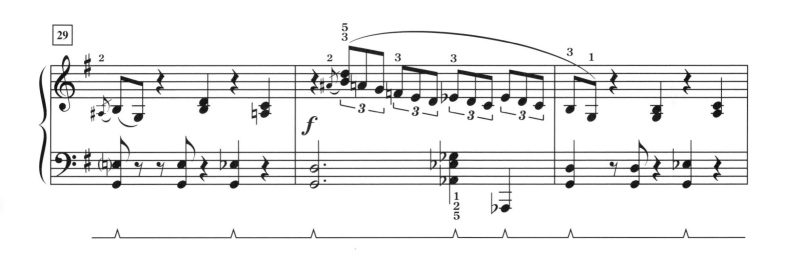

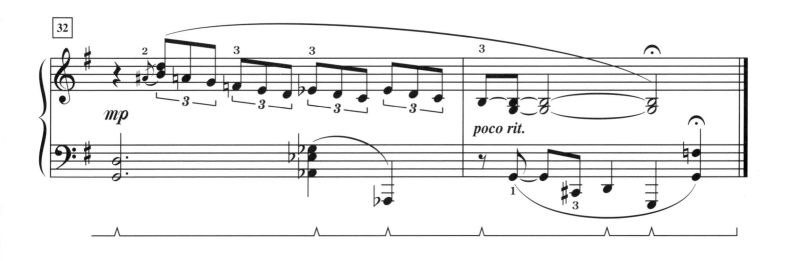

Midnight Waltz

Dennis Alexander

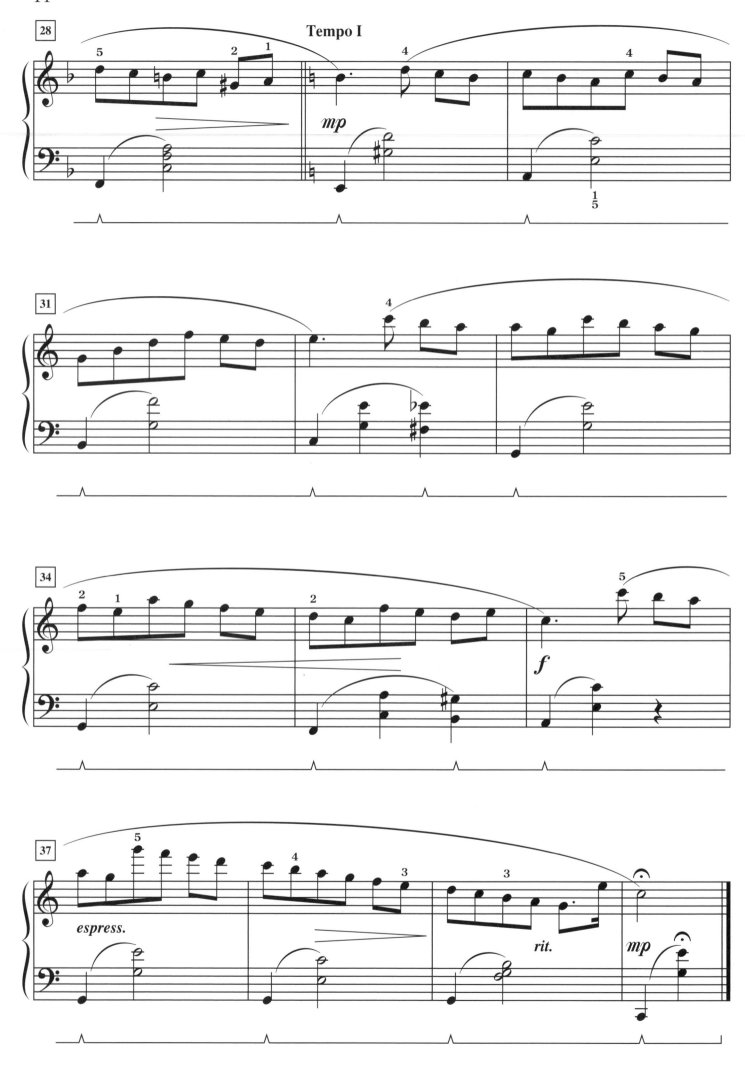

Mountain Mists

Dennis Alexander

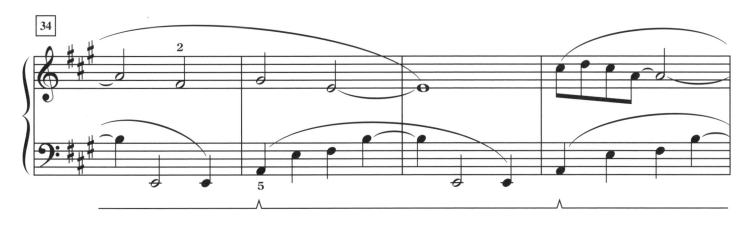

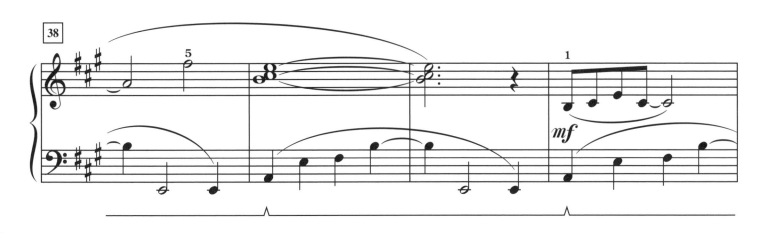

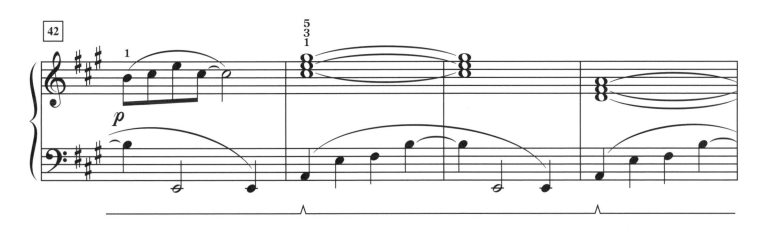

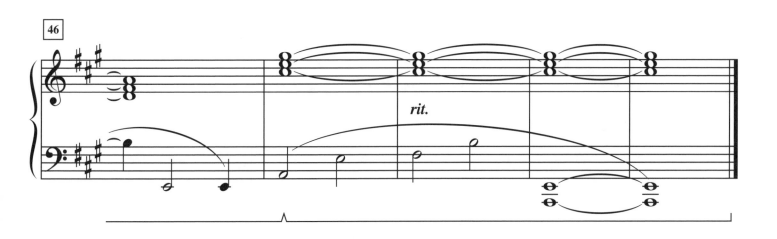

Twirlathon

Dennis Alexander

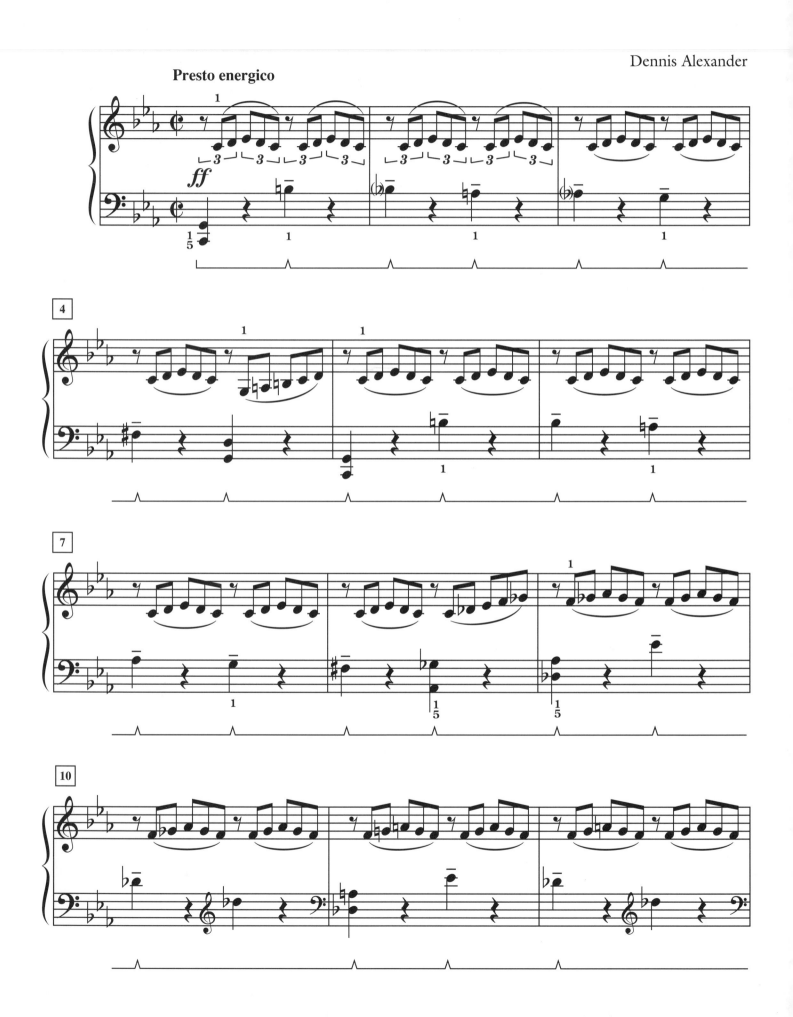

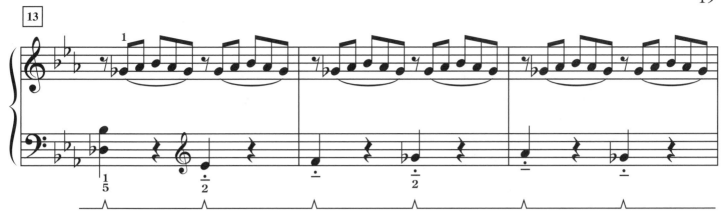

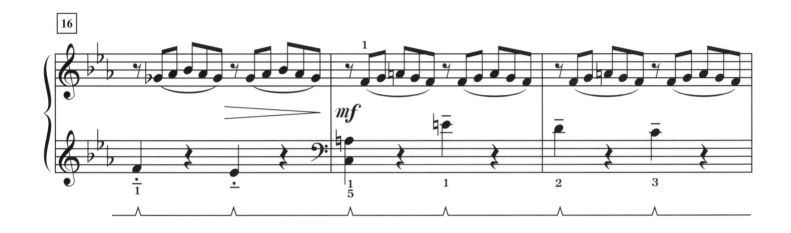

*Students with small hands may omit the top note.

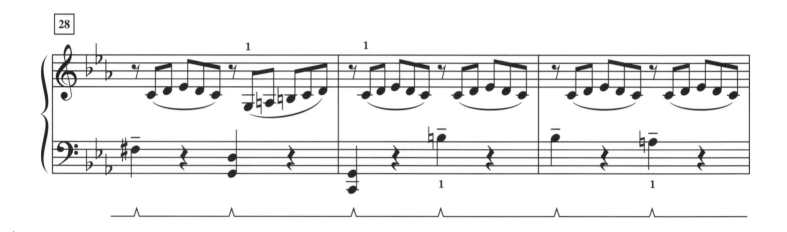

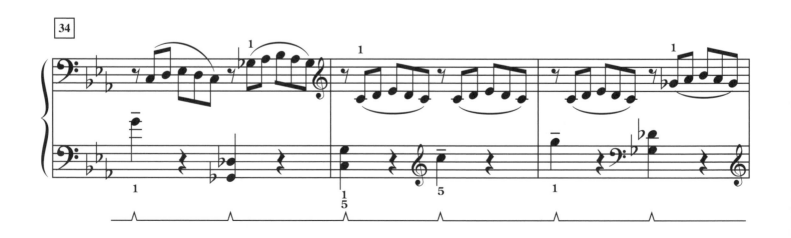

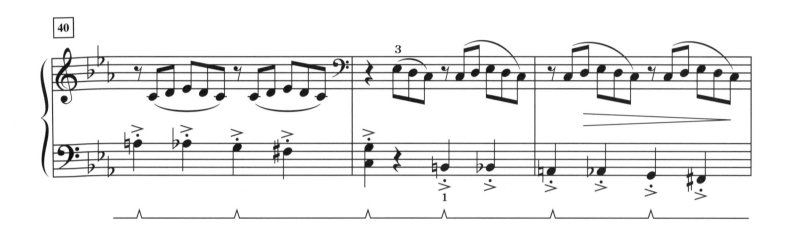

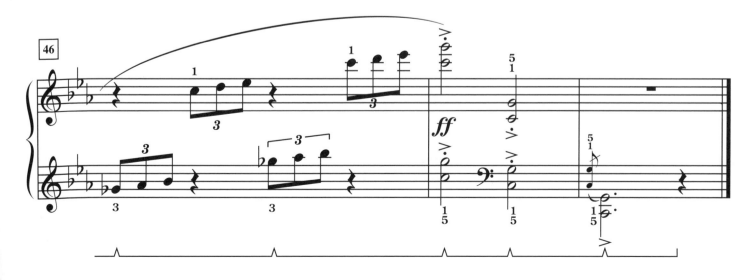

Be Boppin' Boogie

Dennis Alexander

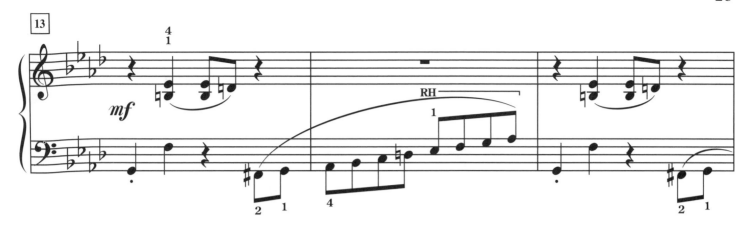

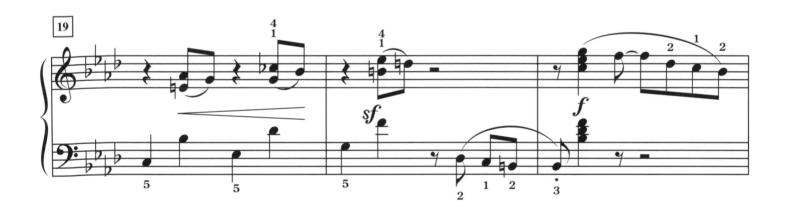

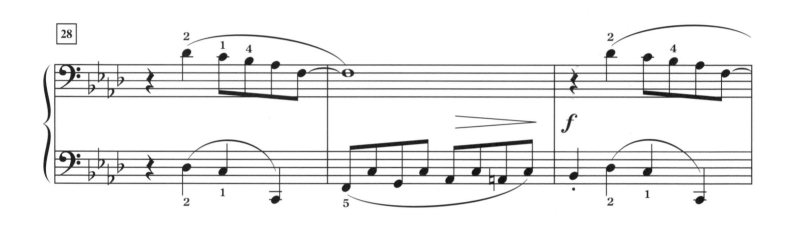

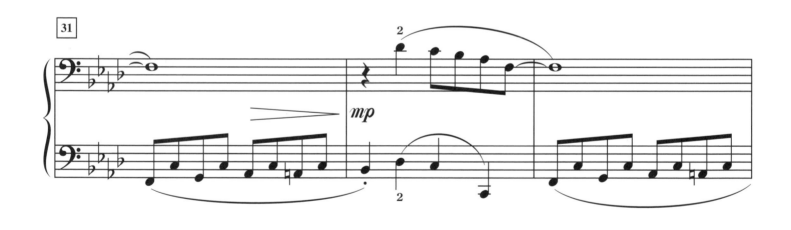

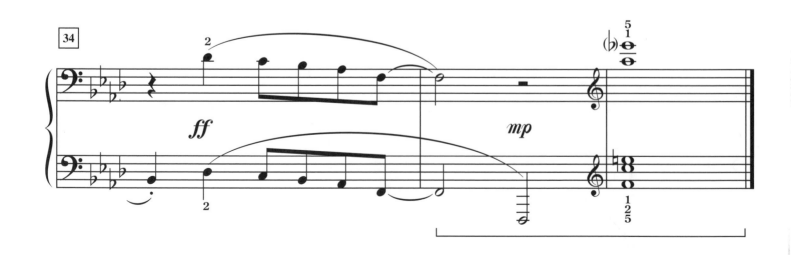

Mary Cassatt (1844–1926). *Mother and Child*, 1900. Oil on canvas, 69 × 51.8 cm. (27⅛ × 20¾ in.). The Brooklyn Museum, Carll H. De Silver Fund.

Berthe Morisot (1841–1895). *Mme Boursier and Her Daughter*, 1874. Oil on canvas, 73 × 56.5 cm. (28¾ × 22⁵/₁₆ in.). The Brooklyn Museum, Purchase.

Thomas Eakins (1844–1916). *Home Scene*, ca. late 1870–71. Oil on canvas, 53.5 × 45.8 cm. (21¹¹/₁₆ × 18¹/₁₆ in.). The Brooklyn Museum, Gift of George A. Hearn, Frederick Loeser Art Fund, Dick S. Ramsay Fund and Gift of Charles A. Schieren.

Paul Gauguin (1848–1903). *Tahitian Woman*, ca. 1891. Pastel on paper, 60.5 × 51.5 cm. (21⅞ × 19½ in.). The Brooklyn Museum, Museum Collection Fund.

1 (outside) Mary Cassatt. Mother and Child, 1900.

3 (outside) Thomas Eakins. Home Scene, ca. late 1870–71.

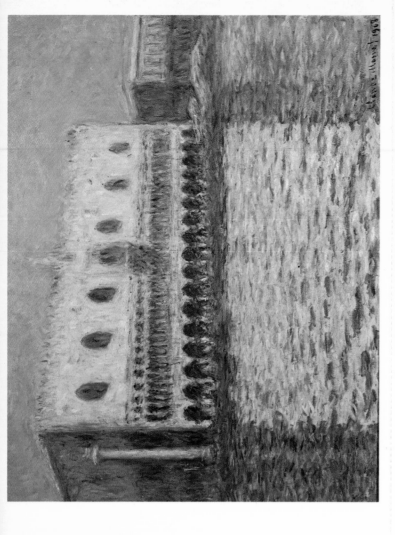

9 (outside) Claude Monet. *The Ducal Palace at Venice*, 1908.

11 (outside) William Glackens. *Bathing at Bellport, Long Island*, 1911.

Paul Cézanne (1839–1906). *The Village of Gardanne*, 1885–86. Oil on canvas, 92 × 74.5 cm. (36¼ × 29⅜ in.). The Brooklyn Museum, Ella C. Woodward Fund and A. T. White Memorial Fund.

Frederic Remington (1861–1909). *The Outlier*, 1909. Oil on canvas, 102 × 69.2 cm. (40⅛ × 27¼ in.). The Brooklyn Museum, Bequest of Charlotte R. Stillman.

Richard Diebenkorn (1922–). *Ocean Park No. 27*, 1970. Oil on canvas, 254 × 205.7 cm. (100 × 81 in.). The Brooklyn Museum, Gift of The Roebling Society, Mr. and Mrs. Charles H. Blatt and Mr. and Mrs. William K. Jacobs, Jr.

Willem de Kooning (1904–). *Woman*, 1953–54. Oil on paperboard, 90.8 × 62 cm. (35¾ × 24¾ in.). The Brooklyn Museum, Gift of Mr. and Mrs. A. Bradley Martin.

Charles Burchfield (1893–1967). *February Thaw*, 1920. Watercolor over pencil, 45.5 × 70.8 cm. (17⅞ × 27⅞ in.). The Brooklyn Museum, John B. Woodward Memorial Fund.

Pierre-Auguste Renoir (1841–1919). *Les Vignes à Cagnes* (*The Vineyards at Cagnes*), 1906. Oil on canvas, 46.3 × 55.2 cm. (18¼ × 21¾ in.). The Brooklyn Museum, Gift of Colonel and Mrs. E. W. Garbisch.

Ernest Lawson (1873–1939). *Garden Landscape*. Oil on canvas, 50.8 × 61 cm. (20 × 24 in.). The Brooklyn Museum, Bequest of Laura L. Barnes.

Hilaire-Germain-Edgar Degas (1834–1917). *Mlle Fiocre in the Ballet "La Source,"* ca. 1866. Oil on canvas, 130 × 145 cm. (51¼ × 57⅛ in.). The Brooklyn Museum, Gift of James H. Post, John T. Underwood and A. Augustus Healy.

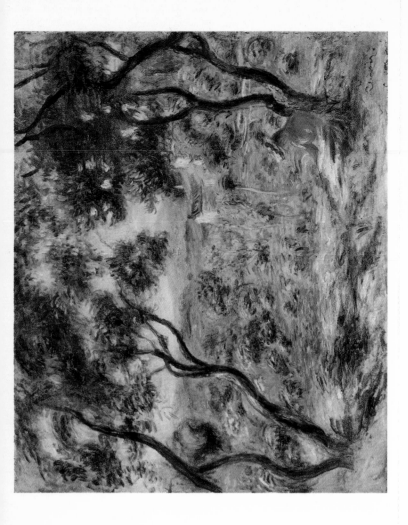

17 (outside) Pierre-Auguste Renoir. *The Vineyards at Cagnes*, 1906.

19 (outside) Edgar Degas. *Mlle Fiocre in the Ballet "La Source,"* ca. 1866.